JIM FAY

ONE — TICKETS TO SUCCESS — ADMIT

Techniques to lead children
to responsible decision-making

The Love and Logic
PRESSInc.
2207 Jackson St.
Golden, CO 80401

Library of Congress Catalog Card Number: 94-76329

ISBN 0-944634-02-8

Printed in the United States of America

Illustrated by
Paule Niedrach Botkin

In his work with families, Jim Fay often meets parents who are like mechanics trying to tune up a car engine—without the proper tools. Jim supplies the proper tools to tune up your relationship with your children.

In Tickets to Success Jim helps you use the basic Love and Logic principles to recharge your family life, and he takes you on a light-hearted trip toward a crucial destination—responsible kids who own and solve their own problems. He's a delightful tour guide.

While you chuckle through Jim's stories, you will be absorbing crucial parenting principles—the principles of shared control, shared decision-making, equal shares of consequences and empathy, and building good self-concepts in children.

If you are new to the Love and Logic principles, here's our golden rule: Kids grow best with a balance of love and logic. Love allows children to grow through their mistakes. Logic allows them to live with the consequences of their choices.

Introduction

Tickets to success are what parents would most like to give their children—tickets that would admit children to the arena of responsible adult life, tickets that would guarantee wise decisions in the real world.

Getting children ready for the real world is our biggest job in our homes and schools. Sometimes we get so tangled up in the curriculum and the pursuit of excellence that we forget to get children ready to deal with the world they'll face when they walk out of the school building after twelve years. That's what this book is all about—getting children ready so that when they get out of school and look out there at the real world, they say "What do you know! It looks just like the one we practiced for!"

I think getting children ready for the real world means making them responsible and teaching them to make their own decisions. Although decision-making is important, it's hard to learn, especially because children rarely get to see how it's done.

How do we adults make decisions? We like to think we base our choices on wisdom and information.

First, we collect data, but our children don't get to see that because it's done inside our heads. Next, we weigh alternatives, but our children don't see that either, because it's also hidden between our ears.

Then we weigh alternatives against consequences, and our children don't see that either. Pretty soon we put a price tag on our decision, asking ourselves which alternative we can afford physically, emotionally, and financially.

Finally, having made our decision, we open our mouths and announce it to the world. And that decision is what our children get to see.

If our children only see adults announcing decisions to the world and have no experience making their own decisions, it's no wonder they seem happy to make decisions with or without information, with or without wisdom.

I believe in giving children experience in making their own decisions, and I believe that their mistakes or misbehavior can provide tickets to success.

During the seventeen years that I was a school principal, I used to wake up in the morning scared to death that some little kid was going to come to school and not misbehave. That may seem a strange thing for a principal to be afraid of, but it's because I really did feel sorry for those nice little kids who came to school every day from kindergarten through sixth grade and behaved themselves. When those well-behaved little kids left school, they didn't know nearly as much about the real world as the children who sometimes misbehaved and had to learn to solve their problems.

By giving our children a chance to make responsible choices and by letting them learn how to solve their problems, we can provide them with tickets to success.

Jim Fay

Chapter

1

Four Steps to Responsibility

The most responsible children I ever saw in my life were the children I had when I was an inner-city school principal. All the children there were from the federal housing projects. Those children would wake up in the morning without an alarm clock and without their parents to help them get over to school for breakfast. Those children knew that if they got there, they got breakfast; if they didn't, they missed it. And they never missed the bus if the bus was going somewhere they wanted to go.

If these children weren't responsible, they went without breakfasts and bus rides.

The most irresponsible children I ever saw in my life were children I had when I was principal in an upper-middle-class suburban school. The first day of school, a thousand children came to school on eighteen different buses. Half of the students went to the playground. The other half went straight to the office telephone.

A stocky first grader said, "I forgot my lunch—You don't want me to go hungry, do you?" (And later his mother drove up with his lunch.)

A third grader with a tennis racket said, "I forgot my warm-up suit. You don't want me to be cold, do you?" (And later his father drove up in a Cadillac.)

A sixth-grade brunette in designer jeans said, "I forgot my registration materials. You don't want me to have trouble, do you?" (And later her papers arrived in a $60,000 sports car.)

If these children forgot food, clothes, or papers, their parents rushed to the rescue.

When I heard those phone calls, I was angry. Those children were being deprived of their opportunities to learn responsibility. You see, I have learned that building responsible children is a four-step process.

1. We give a child a chance to act responsibly.
2. We hope and pray the child makes a mistake.
3. When the child makes a mistake, we stand back and allow consequences, accompanied by liberal doses of empathy, to do the teaching.
4. We give the child exactly the same assignment, offering another chance to act responsibly.

In building responsible children, step three is crucial. Those suburban parents were robbing their children of that ticket to success. I wasn't willing to steal tickets from children.

I announced to the school that children could use the phone any time, with one restriction: They couldn't use the phone to make a problem for anybody else.

The next time the brunette in designer jeans asked to use the telephone, I answered, "No problem. What do you want to use it for?"

"I forgot my homework, and I want my mother to bring it."

"Sorry," I told her. "That's making a problem for your mother."

She told me her mother didn't mind. The truth was that her mother would probably have felt guilty if she didn't deliver the homework. But I held to the rule.

"I mind. And I think it's a problem to put your mother in a cold car, burn her gas, and disrupt her day. No way am I going to have any part of that."

Naturally, the children were unhappy. Then the parents got on my back because their children were unhappy. Eventually I was in danger of losing my job.

I didn't want to lose my job. I enjoyed my work, and didn't like the prospect of losing my house, my car, and my grocery money.

So I wrote a letter to the editor of the local paper.

I wrote something none of the parents could disagree with. I wrote, "The greatest gift I have to give you in this community is building responsible children." That got their attention, because nobody could disagree with wanting responsible children.

I wrote newsletters.

I described the four-step process for building responsible children—giving a responsibility, praying for a failure, allowing consequences with empathy, and giving the same responsibility again.

I gave speeches.

I told parents the story of Brad.

Brad was a fourth-grader at one of the schools where I was principal. On class picture day no one noticed that Brad had flipped the bird when the picture was shot.

No one noticed—until the day finished pictures were in the hands of parents.

The phone calls began. "What kind of school are you running over there?" "What are you teaching in that place?"

Brad, of course, ended up in my office. He told me his teacher sent him and told him not to return to class until he had solved his problem. He knew our problem-solving rule: His solution could not create a problem for someone else.

I asked what his ideas were for solutions. He inspected the floor and said he didn't know.

"Well, that's sad for you, Brad," I said. "It must be hard to have such a big problem and no ideas yet how to solve it."

I paused.

Then I asked, "Would you like to hear what other kids have tried before?" (I asked Brad that question because I have found that children will listen to what other children have tried before, but they won't listen very well to what I've tried or what I think should be done. Then I try to suggest the worst alternative first, because they usually reject the first one.)

Brad wanted to hear.

"Well, some kids call the photographer, and they ask him to doctor the negatives, and reprint the pictures."

Brad was eager. "Oh, I like that! Wish I had thought of that!"

"Don't you want to hear more ideas?"

"No, I want to get it over with." (Oh well, most children reject the first idea, but there are exceptions.)

I went to get the phone number.

While I got the phone number, I made a few calls of my own. One of my rules over the years (after I learned the hard way) was to call the adults first, before the child called, so they would understand what was going on.

I called the photographer. "I don't want Brad to bleed to death, but if we can leave just a tiny little scar, one he can refer back to as he grows up, I think he'll be a better man for it."

I called Brad's mother and described the situation. (When I talk with parents, I use the magic word "describe." It's a word almost all parents will listen to. They get tired of being told.) I asked for her support.

"Brad's going to be calling pretty soon. He has to use the phone. He doesn't know it yet, but it's a long distance phone call. If you could just tell him it's okay to charge the call to home and pay you later, that would support me immensely." She agreed.

Then I took the photographer's number to Brad.

Brad looked at the scrap of paper in his hand, puzzled. "That's a funny-looking number. What's this 1-312—?"

I told him it was a Chicago number.

"Hey, that's long distance!" he said.

I gave him choices. He could pay me cash or ask his mother if it was okay to charge the call to his home number. He had no cash, his mother gave permission, and he dialed the photographer.

He described his problem—his friends wouldn't talk to him, his teacher wouldn't let him back in class . . . Could the photographer doctor the negative?

"Sorry," he answered. "For ethical reasons, I never doctor negatives."

"Oh, no," groaned Brad. "What am I going to do?"

The photographer offered to help. For a $15.00 fee, paid in advance, he would retake the picture on a day he was in town. He would need help unloading his van, and Brad would need the risers set up and the kids standing on them when the photographer arrived. After all for $15, a photographer couldn't do all the work.

Brad was relieved. He could afford $15.

"Of course," the photographer added, "there is the additional dollar charge for each new picture I print."

Brad did some fast mental math. "That's $48! I don't know what to do."

"I thought you'd like the price," said the photographer. "If I can do it when I'm already in town, I won't have to charge you the $638 air fare to bring my equipment from Chicago."

Brad changed his tune. "That $48 sounds like a good price to me. I have $70—my grandma gives me money every birthday and Christmas. I think this would be a good investment."

Brad asked about a date, and turned to me. "Would November 17 be okay?"

"Are you sure you want to do this?" I asked. "There might be something else—"

"No, I want to get it over with."

I cleared the date, and Brad wrote down the information, and hung up. "What do you think I ought to do now?"

"Gee, I don't really know," I said. "Sounds to me as if you have things pretty well in hand."

"I think I'll go to class and tell them I have the problem solved," he said.

As Brad walked down the hall, I thought to myself that it was sad that he was the only child out of 1,120 in that school getting a quality education that day. He wasn't limited to the curriculum; he got to learn about the real world and how the real world works.

Posing for that second picture on November 17, Brad's bird finger never even twitched.

When I told Brad's story to those angry parents at that suburban school, I told them I wanted each of their children to get the same quality education as Brad had. I wanted each of their children to get ready for the real world.

I reviewed with them the steps in building responsible children.

1. Brad had been given a responsibility: posing for the class picture.
2. With a single finger, Brad had failed the assignment.
3. With empathy, I allowed him to live with the consequences: he arranged and paid for the replacement picture.
4. Brad had the same assignment again when the picture was retaken.

I wanted the students who forget lunches, warm-up suits, and registration materials to have their own tickets to success.

Those parents decided to try ticket making. They allowed me to finish out that year, and another, and another . . .

I distributed success tickets at that school for ten years. When students forgot lunches, they went without—or they could choose something from the fruit basket.

Students without warm-up suits missed practice, played in jeans, or got chilly playing in shorts.

Late registration materials carried consequences, too.

I was empathetic. I said, "Gee, that's too bad," but no parent rescued them. The next day they had a second chance to remember food, important papers, and clothing.

Our school was like the real world, and we even set up the circumstances to let children make decisions, beginning in kindergarten.

Chapter

2

Letting Children Make Decisions

As we entered the fall season in the Colorado Rockies, our kindergarten teacher announced at recess, "Guess what? It's decision time. We've got to make decisions about hats, coats, and boots. I think I'll put on my coat. I hate to be cold!"

As her students bolted outdoors, she followed, reassuring them, "Don't worry about your valuable stuff in here. Nobody will bother it—I'm locking the door."

Five minutes later the cold penetrated.

Students said, "We'd better get our coats. It's cold out here."

"That's why I wore mine," said the teacher. "I'm nice and warm."

"Will you unlock the door so we can get our coats?"

"No."

"Why not? You're the boss of our classroom."

"Yes I am, but I'm not going to unlock the door until recess is over."

"Well, what are we going to do?"

"Would you like to hear what some other kids have tried before?"

They did.

She ran through a list, worst choice first, of course. "Some kids go out and cry, and they find out if they cry hard enough it generates heat. Some kids go out and run around, and if they run around hard enough, that makes heat so they feel warmer. Some kids discover it's warmer on the south side of the building, under the balcony where the sun shines on the bricks. Some kids just go out and think real hard about what they are going to do tomorrow. And some kids go out and feel sorry for themselves."

"Does that mean we're not going to get our coats?

"Yeah, it means you're not going to get your coats."

She stayed out five more minutes. (She knew no child ever died outside in five minutes.)

Then she went in and hung up her coat. "I'm really glad I wore this," she said.

She never said a word about the students' coats.

The next day at recess, she announced another decision time and said, "I think today I'll carry my coat with me and hang it on the fence, so I'll have it if I need it . . ."

The beauty of that kindergarten teacher's method was that she always told those students what *she* was going to do. She never told them what she was *not* going to do, or what *they* were to do.

Most of the time kids accept what we say we are going to do. They dig in their heels and put up their fists when we announce what they are going to do.

In a few days the kindergarten teacher noticed something. Each day before recess the kids began asking each other, "How cold do you think it is out there?" They even began sending a representative down the hall to look at the big thermometer, and they were accosting any adult who had been outside, asking, "How cold is it out there? Do you think we need our coats today?"

After a few weeks those kindergartners were also having astounding conversations with their parents:

"Will you teach me to put on these boots?"

"Why?"

"I'm using up most of my recess trying to get them on."

"Why isn't your teacher helping?"

"She says her job is supervising kids."

Before long these kindergartners knew how to zip and button.
They could don coats and pull on boots.

These skills are important in our country today, where parents
are often gone from home before their children. When children
leave for school by themselves, they have to be able to take care
of themselves.

In this school it was especially important, because the school
was located in a small mountain community. In the morning
some of those children left homes at an altitude of 10,000 feet
after their parents had left for work. At such a high altitude,
fall temperatures can be very low in the morning.

The children headed for bus stops that might be a quarter or a half mile away. Those bus stops might be isolated and far from any house or building. The bus might or might not arrive on time, depending on weather conditions. And in those mountains the wind chill factor can drop the temperature from 30 degrees above to 30 degrees below zero in half an hour.

Johnny needs to know that the quality of his life—in fact his life itself—depends on his decisions.

Letting Johnny make decisions can begin even earlier than kindergarten.

And his decisions can affect not only the quality of his life, but the quality of the lives of his parents. Many a father's quality of life has momentarily plummeted while he waited for a preschooler to finish a meal in a restaurant.

When my child goes to the fast-food restaurant with me and dawdles over dinner, I tell her what I will be doing: "My car will be leaving in five minutes."

And I give her a choice. "You can leave in one of two ways: hungry is one way, full is another."

By creating these options, I've set up a winnable war. (If I offer her a choice between eating under her own power and having me force feed her, I'm bound to lose. Preschool jaw muscles are invincible.)

At the end of five minutes, even if her plate is still full, I offer her another choice: "We're heading for the car, and you can go in one of two ways: under your power is one, and under my power is another."

Again I've given a decision and constructed a winnable war. A preschooler's other muscles are less invincible.

If she chooses to use my power, I still have one hurdle left: my need for the approval of the rest of the diners in the fast-food restaurant. I try not to worry about them. Odds are I'm not building a lifelong relationship with any of them.

The real learning for this preschooler comes two hours later when she's hungry.

Then I have choices. (Feeding her immediately is not an option!)

One is to say, "You should have listened to me, but you didn't. That's why you're hungry. Maybe next time you will listen."

The other is to try empathy and say, "For sure, honey. I know how hungry I get when I miss dinner. Don't worry, though. I'll cook you a really big breakfast in the morning because I know how hungry you'll be."

During dinner at Burger Heaven next month, she'll get the same set of choices. And she'll get the same set at a different restaurant the month after that.

Eventually she'll be saying astounding things like, "I'm finished, Dad. How soon does the car leave?"

When we let children make decisions and they get a little cold or hungry, they learn about the real world. If we rescue them, we've robbed them of their tickets to success.

If we yell and scream instead of using empathy, we muddy the water of their decision-making. Instead of yelling and screaming, we can imitate the IRS.

Chapter

3

The IRS Approach
and Affordable Price Tags

The IRS has never yelled at me. Over the past ten years I have been in trouble with that agency twice. Both times the agent told me of my infraction in a gentle voice, concluding softly, "No problem. Your penalty will be due on October 15."

Both times he even gave me choices. "You can pay with cash or your house—either one." But neither agent ever yelled at me. The IRS balances consequences and empathy.

When Brad ruined the class picture, I empathized with his dilemma.

When a preschooler doesn't eat a meal and gets hungry, we're sad for her.

When Susy gets an F in spelling, we're disappointed along with her.

We don't yell.

We don't scream.

And we let the consequences do the teaching.

We don't pay the photographer bill, provide a late dinner, or ask the teacher to change the grade.

We balance consequences and empathy. After all, the IRS doesn't declare amnesty on taxes past due.

It's important to take the IRS approach early, when the consequences have affordable price tags. Learning to watch for traffic when crossing streets and to dress warmly at 10,000 feet are lifesaving decisions, but most foolish choices at the elementary school level have affordable price tags.

I have a friend who is known in her family as "Mom, the Bank." She loves to lend money to her children.

She says she's just like First National, handing out money often. And like First National, she requires promissory notes and collateral. Her children always know when their notes are due and what the collateral is.

She once repossessed a $29 tape recorder from her 10-year-old son.

He's a lucky 10-year-old because it only cost him $29 to learn about fiscal responsibility. He learned about banking, collateral, and repossession, and his lesson had an affordable price tag.

Some kids don't get to learn that lesson until they are 25, and First National repossess their $29,000 4-wheel drive.

Affordable price tags are more than just matters of dollars and cents, though.

If Jill forgets her homework, what's the price tag? She gets a zero in the grade book and tomorrow she can try again.

What if Tom forgets his field trip permission slip? He doesn't get to go. He won't be a permanently disadvantaged student.

And then there's Joey.

Five-year-old Joey calls other children nasty names, especially children who are older, bigger, and tougher than he is.

If Joey's parents let them, these children will teach Joey not to call them nasty names.

It won't be a free lesson. It may cost him a black eye or a few bruises or a bloody nose. And for that price he'll learn to treat bigger and tougher children with respect.

Or Joey's parents can protect him.

They can go with Joey and tell kids to leave him alone.

They can tell his teachers to make sure other kids are nice to him.

If they do this, instead of learning his lesson in respect at 5, he'll learn it at 15. What does it cost to learn that lesson at 15? I know I'd rather have my son learn his lesson at 5 than 15.

Fifteen-year-olds can be pretty nasty.

I'd like children to learn responsibility when the price tags on their success tickets are affordable, and I'd like them to make their decisions based on the consequences, not based on the fear that I will yell at them.

After all, I won't be at the teen bash with them when they decide to chug-a-lug a six-pack.

And I won't be in the back seat of the car to get mad when they decide to drive 90 miles an hour on snowy roads.

I want teenagers who have learned more than algebra and the capital of Alabama in elementary school. I want teenagers who have so much practice making decisions that they automatically ask, "How is this going to affect me?" I want teenagers who have the success ticket of learning to think through consequences during the years of affordable price tags.

Chapter

4

**Getting Children to Own
and Solve Their Problems**

When Brad ruined his class picture, he had a problem, and he solved it. I confess, though, I helped just a tad. I got him to solve his problem with the five steps for problem solving I always use with kids.

1. Show empathy. "That's sad for you," I told Brad.

2. Imply the child is smart enough to solve the problem. "It must be hard to have such a big problem and no ideas, yet, how to solve it." (I implied he would eventually have ideas.)

3. Ask permission to share alternatives. "Would you like to hear what other kids have tried?"

4. Look at the consequences of each alternative. I didn't get to use this with Brad. He leaped in before his cue and grabbed my first alternative—but that's okay. I guide kids through shared control.

5. Let the child decide to solve or not to solve the problem. Brad phoned the photographer. He decided immediately to solve his problem. Some children don't.

These five steps can be tickets to a child's success in problem solving. Let's look at these steps in more detail and watch a few more kids solve problems.

Step 1
Show empathy.

No one in the world is ever going to listen to me until I demonstrate beyond doubt that I understand how he or she feels.

Ricky came to my office from the playground one morning complaining, "The kids are picking on me. They're calling me names and they won't let me play soccer. They never let me play with them."

I empathized. "I bet that makes you feel . . . embarrassed." (As a principal I didn't have lots of time for reflective listening, so I used, "I bet," a phrase I'd borrowed from child psychologists. I tried to figure out what a child was feeling and threw it out following "I bet.")

Ricky nodded. "Embarrassed—and mad."

"Oh, mad. I don't blame you."

Step 2

Give an implied message that says, "You're so capable of thinking for yourself—so powerful, so thoughtful, so intelligent—that I don't have to tell you what to do."

If I say this message directly, rather than implying it, a child will discount my every word. So I imply that he or she is powerful enough to handle the situation.

As Ricky stared at my carpet, I asked him a question adults rarely ask a child, "How do you think you're going to work this out?"

Ricky looked up, shocked. No one had ever asked him that before. It's a statement reserved for two people who really value each other.

"I dunno," he said.

"That's sad for you," I said, "having a big problem and not knowing, yet, what you're going to do about it."

Step 3
Get permission to share alternatives.

When I get permission I ask the one question I've found will get children to listen. I ask if they'd like to hear what other kids have tried before, not what other kids have done, but what other kids have tried.

Before Ricky could begin to study my carpet again, I asked my million-dollar question. "Would you like to hear what other kids have tried before?"

He was starving for ideas.

"Well," I said, "some kids go out and they bust those other kids right in the mouth. There's one idea. (As usual, I put the worst idea first.)

"Some kids go out there and call them names. That's two."

"Some kids go out there and tell the other kids to stop. That's three."

"Some kids go out and get an adult to order them to stop. That's four."

"And some kids go out and express their feelings with "I messages." They say things like, 'Do you know that when I'm picked on in front of other kids I get really embarrassed?' That's five."

"Can you think of any other ideas?"

Ricky couldn't.

Step 4
Look at the consequences of each possible solution.

With a little prodding a child can think through possible results of his choices. He can ask, "What if. . .?"

"How about busting them in the mouth?" I asked Ricky. "I bet that would be fun!"

"Yeah . . . but then we'd all be in trouble," he said.

"Well, then, how about calling them names?"

"Nah . . . They'd just pick on me more."

"Could you just tell them to stop?"

"I already tried it. It doesn't work."

"How about if an adult told them?" I asked.

Ricky liked that. "Yeah! Would you do that?"

I told him I'd be glad to. I had done that before.

"How did it work?" Ricky asked.

I told him that in my office the kids had been very nice, and they had promised not to pick on the boy anymore.

Ricky smiled. "Sounds great!"

I said there was one small problem. "After school they beat up on the boy for telling me."

Ricky ruled out option four.

"That leaves 'I messages'—telling them how you feel," I said.

"I've never tried that before. I don't know . . . " Ricky's voice trailed off.

"I'll let you think about it," I said. "Adults often use 'I messages' to settle problems."

Step 5
Let the child decide to solve
or not to solve the problem.

Letting the child decide feels wrong because we don't get closure. We like closure.

But think about a psychologist. At $100 per hour, he responds with, "Um . . . uh huh . . . oh . . . " and "What do you think?"

When an hour is about up, he asks a really probing question. When you start to answer, he glances at the clock and says, disappointed, "Oh, look at that! Time is up. We'll discuss it next week."

Why? He wants it to rattle around in your head for a whole week.

Our children are better off, too, if their problems are not solved instantly but rattle around in their heads awhile. Time to think is another success ticket we can give them.

So, I concluded my meeting with Ricky by saying, "Pal, there are two kinds of kids in our school. One kind grooves on misery and the other grooves on happiness. I'd feel strange telling a kid to be happy if he would rather be miserable or to be miserable if he'd rather be happy. So guess who gets to decide?"

Ricky raised his eyebrows and put his finger on his chest.

"Right, pal! You get to choose whether to solve your problem or not to solve it, whether to be happy or miserable. Good luck! I hope things work out for you."

With those words I gave Ricky a great gift—the right to make his own decisions about solving or not solving his own problem.

I don't know what decision Ricky made. Principals sometimes need to live without the satisfaction of closure.

But not always.

Although he had to wait for it, grade school principal Charles Turner experienced the bonus of closure in dealing with David.

David was a whimpy redhead with a smart mouth and a mother who spent her life either telling him what to do or rescuing him.

One day she called Mr. Turner to complain. "David's been at your school four years and still doesn't have a single friend. What are you going to do?"

He answered, "I'd like to help. Can you think of anything you haven't tried that might work?"

She couldn't.

He promised to talk with David.

During the conference in the principal's office, David swung his legs back and forth under his chair as Mr. Turner said, "I understand you don't have any friends, David."

"Never had any my whole time at this school."

Mr. Turner empathized. "That's a bummer, David. I've noticed more kids without friends. Kids here don't seem to like much. They don't even like the color of the bricks."

"Never did think they looked good," said David.

The principal let David know he was capable of solving his problem. "What are you going to do about it, David?"

"I dunno," said David.

"That's really a bummer—big problem like that and no ideas what to do. Would you like to hear what some kids without friends have tried before?"

"I guess."

"Doesn't sound like you want to hear, David. I need to know for sure."

David's legs stopped swinging. "Yeah, I want to hear."

Mr. Turner listed some choices kids had tried. "Some kids try to be real nice and tough it out, don't bother anybody with it, and hope it will go away. That's one way. And some kids go to the teacher and whine and cry until the teacher does something about it. That's another way."

"Some other kids go home and whine and cry until their parents call up the school and make the principal do something about it. That's a third way. And some kids get tired of having no friends, so they ask themselves, 'I wonder why I don't have any friends? I wonder who could tell me?' And then they pick two kids who would be gentle and honest and they ask them. And then they decide to either listen to the answer or not listen, depending on what they hear."

At the end of his list, Mr. Turner asked, "Can you think of anything else, David?"

David couldn't. He then rejected ideas one through three. He had tried them already.

His back straightened at suggestion four. "I don't have to try that!"

"Right, David. You don't have to." Mr. Turner escorted David to the door. "Good luck."

As David walked through the doorway, he shook his head, confused. As Mr. Turner watched him trudge down the hall, he felt like a deflated balloon. As principal, he had no sense of closure.

But two weeks later David rushed through his office door. "I know two guys. I know two guys who'll be gentle and honest!"

"Do you want to bring them to my office?"

"Yeah."

He brought them. The three sat in silence.

Finally David said, "Well, aren't you going to ask them?"

"I wasn't planning on it, David. I have plenty of friends." (Mr. Turner didn't tell David the problem was his, he simply implied it. Implication is more effective.)

Then he helped out just a bit. "David picked you guys because he thinks you can be gentle and honest and he wants to ask you a question."

David picked up his cue. "Why don't I have any friends?"

They told him.

One said, "Gee, David, the way you act, you can't have friends. You hassle us at recess, and in class you knock stuff off our desks. When we try to get even, you tattle to the teacher, and we get in trouble. Kids don't like a guy who gives it out, but can't take it."

The other boy said, "David, you think you're too good for us."

David protested, "I do not!"

"Yes, you do. You never play with us. Instead of playing soccer you stand against the building."

"But I want to play. I . . . I'm scared to ask."

"Gee, David. Around here, if you want to play, you play. You don't ask!"

Silence fell. David had no more questions. He excused the boys and stayed seated, looking forlornly at Mr. Turner.

"What's the matter, David?"

"I don't know."

"It sounds as if you want me to tell you what to do, David. I don't do that. Want to know why?"

David did.

Mr. Turner told David about his right to choose happiness or misery, depending on which he preferred. Then he wished David good luck.

Again, Mr. Turner's sense of closure was delayed, but only until student council elections the following fall.

David was elected fourth grade council representative.

Mr. Turner had done his work well. He had empathized, offered alternatives, and let David choose.

He could have blown it. He could have said, "David, these two guys gave you good information. Now go and do something about it."

David probably would have said to himself, "I can think for myself. I'll do just the opposite of what you want."

A teacher named Mrs. Ogden used the five steps to help a ninth grader solve the problem of a poor report card.

Paula stomped up to Mrs. Ogden's desk after school on report card Friday, exclaiming, "Look at this awful report card, Mrs. Ogden—3 F's, a D and a C. I can't take this home. My parents will take me out of basketball!"

Mrs. Ogden wanted to lecture—"You earned the grades, so face the music."

Instead she said, "That's a bummer. It's really sad for you, Paula. What are you going to do?"

(Note the empathy and the implied wisdom.)

Paula didn't know, so Mrs. Ogden asked if she'd like to hear about some options. Paula did.

(Note the request for permission to share alternatives.)

Mrs. Ogden offered several suggestions. "Some kids burn the report card. Some kids lie and tell their parents they don't get report cards this semester. Some get their friends to change the grades. Some kids try bossing their parents around about the report card."

Paula didn't think that she wanted to do any of these, so Mrs. Ogden offered, "Some kids actually try using the truth. That often blows parents away. But, Paula, I've run out of ideas. Good luck."

Paula looked skeptical as the teacher concluded, "I'd better get back to my work. I hope you can work it out with them."

(Note that Paula got to decide on her own solution.)

The next Monday morning Paula ran up to Mrs. Ogden's desk, waving a signed report card. "Guess what? I blew them away with honesty. I was awesome! "

"I took that report card home, threw it on the kitchen table and yelled, 'Look at this lousy report card. Boy, have I learned my lesson.' I pointed my finger at them said, 'You guys better do something about this!'"

"You were right, Mrs. Ogden! Parents don't like to be bossed around. And they sure can't handle honesty. They were so blown away, they didn't even take me out of basketball!"

At last report, Paula's grades had improved significantly, and her parents were still shaking their heads in amazement.

The problem of the bad report card, combined with Paula's agonizing over dealing with her parents was a sufficient consequence in this case. These wise parents didn't resort to overkill. Had Paula's grades not improved, they could have gone a step further.

Given an opportunity to solve their own problems, David and Paula made first-rate decisions.

I used to believe that children always made second-rate decisions. Now I know why so many children make bad choices. Often we adults take ownership of the good choice, and we tell children they should choose that one.

They don't, of course. Because of their need for some sense of control, they make a bad choice. Their need for power is stronger than their need to make a good choice.

I believe that when a child is given a full range of choices from bad to good, he or she will invariably choose a good one. He or she will act responsibly.

Raising responsible children is our greatest objective as teachers and parents. Responsible children own tickets to success.

But children are not born responsible. They learn responsibility as we allow them to make decisions and to live with the consequences.

In the end, we cannot give children tickets to success. There is no free lunch, no free ride, and no free ticket. Day by day, choice by choice, decision by decision we can allow our children to earn their tickets to success.

Conclusion

We adults have a choice, too.

We can pressure children into bad choices by owning the good ones, or we can let them make wise choices by offering them a full range of choices.

We can yell and lecture, or we can empathize.

We can rescue them from a mistake, or we can allow them to learn from the consequences.

Well pal, I'd feel strange, telling you what to do.

So guess who gets to decide?

Right!

Good luck.

Hope it works out for you.

. . . And for your children.

The Author

Jim Fay, with over 30 years experience in education, is one of America's most sought-after presenters and consultants. Jim's "Love and Logic" philosophy has revolutionized the way parents and professionals work with children. He is the author of over 90 books, tapes and articles on parenting and positive discipline.

Call today for a free catalog of our complete line of Love and Logic books and audio and video tapes.

1-800-338-4065